black

on

white

s e e d s

a

d i s h

shira dentz

Shearsman Books
Exeter

Published in the United Kingdom in 2010 by
Shearsman Books Ltd
58 Velwell Road
Exeter EX4 4LD

www.shearsman.com

ISBN 978-1-84861-128-3
First Edition

Acknowledgements
See pages 92–94.

Cover design by the author
Author photo by Cris Baczek

for my brother, Asher
...

contents

•

• •

• • •

• • •
   •

• • •
   • •

"the appetite

for comfort went looking,
inner, tonal,

for where the green begins"
Fanny Howe

"A thousand needlesful of green & blue thread"
Francis Ponge

●

The Grasses Unload Their Grief

Our feet didn't touch the ground all year, but we marched, gray
smoke, one leg following the other curved like scythes, turning with
the measure of blades rippling in a field.

The three of us our skin removed laid away like winter covers
from a bed. Underneath wasn't flesh, bone or blood, though all
our organs kept.

I could see right into my mother and father. In each of their
mists a coiled chain. Then, shame or no shame, I knew I looked
the same only smaller.

A son, a brother.

By the time we slipped back into our bodies, the chain had
shrunk like an umbilical cord.

Instead of words, my mother uttered syllables that fit onto silver
teaspoons whose glossy oval backs flew into the sky.

Instead of words, my father blew cinders.

The Wind of Madness Has Broken a Skin

Something at the edge of danger
Turns into its opposite, and circles:

Frigid wind, now blue flame,
Curls a rind out of the night's air.
Black space a springy trampoline.

The void is unusually still, like a lake
With nothing pulling on it.

Mania's headdress
Is a thin, lilac gauze.
The back of her toes (as well as the cracks between)
Are wiggling ligatures disassembling.

Whirlwind upon whirwind upon whilwind,
A petal falls off the black-mum sky.

Mania's many heads wheel around.
A spider sticks to her mind. Not something she knows.
She's only hanging the receiver from the pay phone on the windiest hill.

The day after is colorless as Antarctica. Trees static at forty-five degrees.
Just before sunset, the landscape straightens.

The pink that rubbed off my bedspread onto my pants
Has rubbed off on a cloud.
Chinese sounds are snow shovels.
French vowels, water sullied the color of cheap topaz.

**The Night Is My Purse,
and Here's What I Empty Out:**

S   ph   r,
the word, *sahphar*—
Hebrew for count,
my father, saying it;
His lips, its sound,
thin as the line in the horizon.

One coin.
The root of *sahpha*r
also means tell.

Sahphar. A head,
a tail. *Seepehr.*

The Root, Three Consonants:

1. Samach (ס) =
    An empty eye socket + a brow overhanging =
    the orifice of my oracular father; and
2. Pai (פּ) minus a dot = Phai (פ) =
    The scowl creasing his face,
     branding him;
     a curlicue that skims
3. Raish (ר) =
    A bended line going in two directions forever;
    his voice streaming

An Index of IDs:

Father, Daddy; My father, Him; The man with no name,
The man with no title, The man with no
nomenclature; Nomenclatureless,

You Know Who
Unpursed Lips, Mementos:

My own piece of nightdark plucked
from a piece that had risen dense
like a drape above my bed:
a kind of headboard.
Something that felt eternal,
something to count on.

Cupid and His Twin Sister:

An Eskimo girl, my first friend—
wearing a polkadot snow jacket,
fleece around her hood.

The constellation Mania and Her Many Heads,
wearing the lilac headdress that changes her into Ophelia.

Her thighs covered in blue jeans.
I want to climb them, the honeysuckle.
She skids like a shadow and disappears into a wall.

Snap,
An insect doing pushups on a stalk of grass.

Getting Closer to the Big Bang

Instead of music, light; instead of sections of instruments, sections
of time. A gamma ray perceptible for 40 seconds that originated
12 billion years ago. A man loses his job after 20 years, the
mailroom guy. And what about ads on the subway saying, *You choose
your presidents—why not choose your cable company?* The heads of
Washington, Jefferson, Lincoln in stone, like the Sphinx. Who,
exactly, had the vote back then?

Creak in an empty car like cracking knuckles, an ash falling on
the ground; swallows of a clock, the *this is a test of the emergency
broadcasting system* tone everpresent in the background; soda fizz
twinkling like stars, a man stepping on the floor above.

Pick particles from sounds, watch phrases rise overhead. When my
brother died I was 8, and wanted to write a requiem to the universe,
even if it lasted only 40 seconds.

Limn

I felt the painting return when the phone rang and I was called upon
        to speak.
My arms stiffened in its rectangle.
Perched in a mad dash, not yet set flat against the wall.
(The thing itself merely expedient: early Renaissance,
a portrait of a woman with long, wavy, chestnut hair.)
The vibration of my voice within the frame tilted the painting
hither and thither.

Only in the flap of hindsight a glimpse
of what I had been: the exposed wall,
whatever holes, smudges and patches were made over time
(the visual equivalent of the sea in a shell),
where safes are rumored to be.

Flowers have lips—their petals,
dispersing phrases as they die.
What's left is a hum, then
silence: black boxes in a crossword.

Amnesia pedals up a lake, takes its place in a grassy swamp
where the most weightless of insects twitter.

Numbness and shade

Voices supple as leaves in their prime,
drying here and there, unstemming,
partitioned into heaps before
decomposing.

The odor of burnt rubber. Spicepackets of my father talking.
Some words are elastic, pale rubberbands
in the mouths of people who produce extra-amounts of saliva.
"I don't find contact with you satisfying anymore,"
writes a friend whose husband is a hanging ivy.

My eye fuzzy as a shopwindow at Halloween.
A cobweb answers the doorbell.
The old lady who lives inside my eye crochets a shawl.
She huddles in it now.

The Existing Lover in Everyday Life

I will appreciate disconnected bits of form

Leaves closing prayerfully
        wings
              a duck wading
A swarm of birds revising its character
like a flame

Origami

The back of our daily parts
is raw hide.
I don't like public spaces.
Colors squirrel into the glass,
the shape of.

Everyone lined up
to get a seat on the mammoth bird.
People flew on its wings,
which were orange crushed-velvet.
They folded, unfolded, and refolded.

**Rorschach: Last week, the moon dipped close to the gray streets,
a surprise guest, huge and yellow.**

Antique, fully exposing its marks (*a man,* they say).
In my dream people were tipping their Future hats to it.
Briefly, I saw the night sky as a place
like a garden,
and things were looking back.

*

Had to feel love for the dead mouse to
get rid of it. *It was a baby.*

*

Thought I'd start with.
Thought I'd learn about distance.
Everyone's eyes are a particular kind of light,
and it was during a shower,
the milky light of a north pole sun in my eyes,
that I recognized yours.

*

Building a dictionary of definitions on your body.
First, your space—an omission.
In hindsight, a shadow sprouts; draped casually as a sock
you might have left behind.

Brushstrokes, India ink,
a print that's *you*.
From tangles of dark and light,
shapes supple as leather.
And I will arrive:
homunculus-like, inside a shoe,
riding its contours.

*

I'm lost in *M*,
the twin, repeating
sound.

                    *

Logs crackling now, spitting.
Built a fire but a small flue and not enough attention
has made a lot of smoke
instead of the animal
I wanted to be companion—

Last night the flame worked.
Fire's an addiction: once you start one up you want it to keep going.
Soon the Fire Department will arrive; I'm ready,
only a matter of time till a neighbor calls them.

In a city, failure can't be a private matter.
Sweaty, learn my lesson:
No no, I won't do it the same way again.

                    *

Butterfly, or insect?
The spine separating the vulva's
two wings,
the hyphen in bisexuality

a woman, a man,
whose hearth

cherry round, red sweet,
banana, also sweet

                    *

Embers.

                *

And now for this man-
love freshly shedding
a petal,   suspended,
decontexted . . .
smell it?

and between women
[pulp of a flower]   brackets are the magnets
andro][ny   violet fire courses through an arm

                *

Overnight
I implant myself a new heart.
Morning, I see the old one:
two pieces, brown and gummy.
Terrified, I shroud them with a towel.

*

Before one of our dates,
I bike once around the park.
Run into a steel wire, keep going.
Told you!, two guys shout at the guy who's been stretching it across
        the road.

Home, look down to untie my sneaker,
see fishing wire and a red brown ten-inch worm dangling
from the bottom of my sweatpants.
What to do? Kick a leg out, *chah, chah,*
but the worm doesn't fall any farther.
Close in on the situation, think, *the mouse.*
A fishing hook's clawed into my pants, pierced into the worm's body.
Try to turn it out, but too jammed. Take the pants off,
don't look at the worm while I envelop it and the pants
with a trash bag.
Later someone says, *It's lucky you were wearing pants.*

*

What I thought were clouds
are covers out of anything
makeshift:
shirts, curtains, old rags.

*

Glimpse you in black,
playing "shapes" in a garden,
a mime artist.
Cultivating aloofness, as if it were a plant with crisp, sharp leaves.

*

You came to stay with me this morning
an unmoving cock;
beached.
Maybe it swelled to capacity
inside my hull;
you let it linger
so I could say goodbye.
In the background the ocean
substituted for rocking.

You've no idea where you've been this morning,
so I can't tell you, thanks.
I do as you bid to let
your curled mollusc slip out.

*

A husk with the indent of your ridges.

*

Ahead, two logs upright in the fireplace,
sculpture from my last attempt.
Brown gray and black in the spots
where the fire caught.

Birdsong

Longing: a talk bubble, yanked out overhead.
Nest shaped.
Twig and whatever leaves go into its making.

How do I explain the cage on my head,
some of the poles spread widely enough
for me to put my wings through,
but not the rest.

：

spoke

in the whirr of the tire
the spokes move so fast
you they

blend into one of the tones
on the gray scale
but not quite

once in a while a metal flash
a line—

takeoff

bicycle wheels   steel spokes   black tires
spin:
you can race off on your blue, the blue

frame behind, wings off   a thunderbird
      whirled wheels,
blue your brother
gone, missing, lost, who

was the bike bought for, you girl
or him?
both of you together
like the whirr of the tire.

      •

      •

Gone, like a cuff link.
Creaselines on my father's forehead,
Duane Reade's fluorescent lights.
A crocus blossom cracks through.

Creaselines on my father's forehead.
A sunflower yolk falls down sleep's chute;
springtime in the unconscious.
A blazing, yellow circle.

A sunflower yolk falls down sleep's chute.
Seeds flung back over my shoulder.
A blazing, yellow circle.
Gone, like a cuff link.

Ribs

In the distance
Between five spread-out fingers
Five years make a hand

Between rusty red poles
of a bridge:
my body cribbed
from falling on the highway underneath.

He's a spirit now.

I look for him
when we pass boats,
wooden tables, the sign "Wonderland."

Photographs

It was important to see him without them. The big cupcake that school gave out on birthdays that he saved an entire afternoon to share with her; the Abraham Lincoln book he brought home from the hospital library; the name of a girl, *Candy*, he met there. A charcoal blue wool hat, the matching scarf with small snowflakes sewn onto his snowsuit, the dresser drawers that were his. The carnival horses wallpapering their room: how she'd hold the lines of their contours in her eyes, then, as if they were pickup sticks, let them scatter; however they'd land she'd see, at the very least, one brand new figure. She made believe it was deliberate, that she was the artist who'd drawn the figure, and look away determined to see it on the wall again; each and every time she'd lose its whereabouts. Their yelping at pigeons in the tunnel they passed through on their way to the supermarket, their voices coming back two, three times, in different shades; the black, plump birds would move a little. But not the sound of his voice nor his way of talking; not his laugh either. The shape of his nails were different from hers; she reconciled their difference by deciding his were boy's. She didn't care for his thumb—it was particularly wide. She tried to find something good about his thumb. Shapes on people's bodies told things. Their width was like the width of a smile. Must have been something very fine about his smiling, especially with his lids purple-black, their sheen like that of worn cloth; in a very short time, too short to notice beginning, his head got bigger, his five-year-old face pocked with teenage acne; a midget man-boy. The Florida t-shirt their grandmother brought back for him was *extra-large*. He became more and more distant—shapes on him changing and rearranging.

-TUDE

Any minute the phone could ring

(Not that I'm expecting anyone) just any moment it could

. . . So, turn the ringer off? Logic goes colloquial, smooth as a

language fin around alabaster. Why not pull purple from the vying

colors of leaves out my back window (upon whose sill my phone rests)?

As twilight darkens the colors quiet and I wonder was it all in my

head . . .

A tiny but collected redhot summer sun is the answering machine's ON.

At night, once I swing into its optical orbit I can safely reach

the bathroom.

There are porches out back. I want one. What's it smell like? Porch

green, I mean. Personal green. Not all gardens are leapsome—especially

at dusk and after.

The exposed circuitry of green gets rerouted,

and green becomes white walls all the better to see the corners where

they converge.

What's wrong with a little artificiality?

What's it like to be paralyzed from the waist down . . . and go places on

your own? For a long time I feel his body as mine. Against the root of

me, he makes an)mb. I swear somewhere something's resonating, only taste the smell of burnt rubber in which copper has smoldered. Sense

out of tense. When he asks me for a program I go to get water ask do

you want some, bring it/then he says—I have tremors, too, so you—.

I hold the cup to his mouth a total stranger but here I am playing

a fountain. While he recites poems by heart (his voice sweaty as he

tries to make it stand, cast as if it were natural light) I look around

in a flurry think I don't want him (or everyone) to think I feel sorry

for him; imagine his bravery rooted as a tree trunk and the particular

play of light and shadows of its leaves as he resolved to come here.

A surreptitious glance down at his feet—limp, bandaged in velcro to

his electronic chair. Later he pushbuttons his way out the door but

can't angle just right so I ask can I help. He says ah yes, I need energy,

could you give me some cheese. I quiver with the orange square

but soon into his eating I remember we should PAUSE for him to

swallow before making any more orange

disappear.

———

The EAST RIVER is pudding on its back. Especially when it

glistens. Out the window on the D-train crossing the Brooklyn

Bridge I see the river's skin, like the way it looks but wouldn't want

to eat it. All the tops of pudding I skimmed off as a kid come to lie around the river now. But with the river, the texture difference between surface and inside is probably an illusion; wouldn't they taste the same, except for temperature and wind?

It's too hot and the windows need to stay wide open and besides trees, leaves, and porches (birds dogs crickets) in the back there's a commercial street, a traffic light (when it's red sudden jolts of RAP) and a public park/playground in the front.

I play a game: Ugly Sounds. A bus sound becomes a gray sidewalk, a gray that's become relentless as a desert. Car alarm?

A wind chime, glass hitting on glass, going all day, somehow talking to my ears, taking the splinters out before they lodge in deep.

This afternoon live love music's in the park and someone announces every five minutes into his megaphone: "The biggest flea market in Brooklyn is happening on 4th Avenue. We have 190 tables set up and food for you all. Come in and enjoy."

A motorcyclist just tore down the street thinking he was a hornet. Cars as waterfalls. Try Bouquet of Sounds.

———

I put a record on:

The Rise and Fall of Trucks Rushing Past My Father and Me on the Highway.

It was made a long time ago. Their Exhaust Fumes.

A great big sigh. Inhale, exhale. The trucks did it for me.

The trucks were like eagles, or cranes; or priests. Because with my father between us nothing could be said.

(twitching halo)

Guilt flickers like a loose fluorescent tube,

I bring him closer to eclipse.
Still the penumbra,
the teeth of fire ringing.

My father is a star:
not in the sky or a picture of,
not as in rock or a movie—
one that has no relationship with space;
in other words, prepositions escape

Shore.

A quick *but*
has taken a biblical forty years to line up.
A telescope in three pieces
that assembles in a pause:

He crackles spits fireballs lashes
for some time I turn
the other cheek.

In the distance, off and on,
a red-hot twister,
three spiraling arms
extend, reverse.

I carry

clubs at my back. A number of feelings draw up seats around the
dinner table.

The top of the river looks like silk. And I forget your barbs, thorny stems.
Vowels fall downstairs, scrambled in storage.

Some people like to find unassociated bits of things and put them together.
To speak is to cross onto a highway.

What does my brother, lifeless, look like? His body steady in the landscape
a shaft of wheat in a field.

Don't you hear the shore, loud as sun, calling this in, that out of time?

"The lock of loss rattles in a wind against which memory has no shelter"

The Importance of Being Earnest

When verbs first rose to leave, it was for periods. I had no idea the
        matter was a part of speech when
arms could be tables; the crest of a wave, gooey.
To begin with, they didn't just fly off;   no,

they were a flutter of birds.
Gradually there was no distance between shades of periods, and the
        stolid period itself.
Their lapses spread to clauses, picking entire sentences clean like
        leaves from trees; dry looks hairy
against a background of pink winter sky.
Every vista brought on a question.
Imagine being a kid in a playground and the sky between everything.

/   /   /   /

I faded illegible as a fly wing.
Why?/ stayed in my gut, indigestible.

In the end they couldn't escape gravity, they sank
underground. Pushing out spaces between letters, becoming infinitely
        obese,
albeit printless.

A letter like the sky seems to stop being a thing once it's no longer
        blue.

This moment ghosted verbs are on an up escalator, circulating like
        carts on a ferris wheel,
perhaps on their way down they'll clasp with their language?

When I was little I had cars with silver balls you placed in them to
go
I compared the balls to energy: (souls)
Feel
feel

I'm a fish, with a beautiful apostrophe.

Here

Singing *I wanna hold your hand*
with my brother, and holding hands.
My own thoughts, thumping in me like a heart.

The sound of the mixmaster, yellow and lumpy.
"Boo!" always moved pigeons.
Wanting more than anything to make music,

for concertos to open their wings from my hands.
My father's davening voice: plains, cliffs, precipice;
operatic, I suppose.

An anonymous male voice: "Ahhh" loudening
by increments into infinity,
scaring me, waking me up.

A 3rd grade teacher reading <u>An Enormous Egg</u>
outdoors; beginning spring,
E.

The sound of Hebrew, foreign and mysterious.
No music, except on the car radio.
Kids' voices: "Ma!," "No!," basketballs clanging

on metal hoops; turning sounds,
like jump ropes coming through the window.
The vowels of my brother after dying.

Chantilly Lace

i.

Raw linen the tinge of yellow-gold   Antique lace
French vanilla ice cream   The way the moon is tonight

Häägen dazs vanilla   Swiss lace   Curtains with pindot holes ruffling
You, in an Elizabethan collar   white   thin   almost not there
Accordion style around your neck,
Prim, trim,
Victorian.

The end of a love affair has the extravagance
Of a wedding: so much cream,
Fabric, reams and reams.

I liked your white: a prism beam
Of violetbluegreenyelloworangered.
I told you so at the beginning,
Before you went to Europe, sent me white roses,
"To more white," the card read.

Pay attention to what happens to the color when it fades—
                              Like old scotch tape

ii.

The way the moon looks tonight

In your little white capsule:
White sheets, feather pillows,
And out the black frame of an uncovered window
The glaze of a winter white sun.
A leg, a tree branch,
Snow powdering on its way down,
Making love a snow dance.

iii.
An emblem:
My father's chalky fingers.
It was their duty to go rough, a custom
Like pulling a sailor's tie tight on a young boy's neck.

He's moving to another country
And wants to know if I'll see him.

Small, I passed him bags of chocolate to weigh.
Tall, helped haul boxes of pizza crusts from a freezer large as three
      rooms,
Strung creamy slats to make venetian blinds,
And steadied panes of glass while he cut them to size;
Now I hear his voice the first time in ten years.

His hands   Two fists   Caulk to me
Sad and swirling, yellow as a healing shiner.

The way the moon looks tonight
Prayer-shawl jaundice.

the undershirt

you
a bay   in the morning.

but last night,   moving pictures:
    first I saw you in your white sleeveless undershirt
            I loved you in that thing   your shoulders
                            mountains encircling a lake

Concert

Stairwell, several steps missing—Gold satin pants, creasing at her
triangle as she sings—light sculpting her hip, thigh—her voice
stretching from that wishbone—Your wishbone, hard and muscular—
like your boxy head

You say, *miss you*   *am in you still*
and someone else   *this is possible*

Clamp the wings butting wings butting wild in a jar—bitter white—
She's on stage in gold satin pants—You in another woman's bed—me,
coughing—I dance,   danced with you,   wine in my legs.

To the New Lover

A rustle whooshes leaves on branches,
charms tinkering on a bracelet.
Sky, in place of leaves,
this shiny afternoon.

You finally got your passion: A woman
with the panache of a gay Frenchman,
3 blue early-autumn days,
trees in full bloom—
setting the table just for you.

You teem with each other's fluids,
inhale her cologne (Jil Sander's *Feeling Man*).
She perches strawberries and grapes on your teeth,
watches your tongue flip them back.
The shadow behind you
twins with hers, bouncing when you
walk to uncork another bottle of wine.

A spacious loft,
private enough to join her soprano with your tenor
when she comes.

I fold a card in two
from a bouquet
she sent early in our romance,
pitch it to the trash.
Tired of cutting, burning,
chopping.
Her gestures, at first, are so exorbitant.

*Caught between her thighs
in her*

Outline of my head,
down to the narrow of my neck
elongates:
like a fetus head,
disproportionately large

A mirror of the shape of her sex
(a spectacle Bosch would have painted)
Am wearing her womb on my head

When she untwines from you
to lie with a new lover,
she'll say, how medieval it is
not to forgive betrayal.

Its skeleton extends to me like a finger.

1.

The other day your voice smelled like suede
and left an imprint—two shallow marks of deer hooves.

Want to call again but you're sealed behind doors, playing opera:

A tree waves.
A string of sunlight rolls out along a moving branch.
A bow sweeps in a tree.

2.

Okay, I have to reconstruct you.
Boxy head, thick neck, nails like seashells.
Thumb angled backwards even in a state of rest. Read: *prone to action.*
What comes next, lips or eyes?
Your black silk shirt and vanilla skin.

Each subway pole I lean against while waiting for the train has
            nipples.
Painted-over bolts like giant strips of candy buttons.

Your tongue, soft and worn as oriental carpets,
parts open my mouth.

3.

Want to touch contours on the phone:

Your pauses familiar
as your basin-shaped derrière.

Voice the only touch can make now.
My mouth an oval of sap,
a hive.

4.

I clean as if you're coming back.
Clean as if when you come back
it's proof I've changed.
Dusting, mopping,

each time I see dust, I think of you.
Each time I smell must.
Each time I see my messy drawers
and clothes wrinkling.

5.

Halfway now
floating across the floorboards,
gleams of light where you passed through.
It's just the swirling path of dark-stained wood.
Half of me moon facing space,
half of me turned toward you.

6.

A new tube of toothpaste measures how long you're gone.
Got a new haircut. Pulled out my sweatshirt.
Used the green towel we sat on for your bon voyage.
All I remember is the blue sky. It was late afternoon

or even later, maybe there wasn't a blue sky,
but that's what I remember, except for the towering
blue fir.
You were taking one last great slumber
like a lick closing an envelope.

I had to sleep with her in order to realize how much I love you, you said.
Look, I said, *that building looks like a castle
cut off by trees.*

7.

Midnight you call saying, *I miss you.*
Why are you sleeping with her, I say.
You tell me the phenomenology of love according to Hegel,
      Heidegger and Foucault.
Something about desiring, the desired, and absence.

Your smell missing from my shirt.
This Saturday I threw out the shaker with the sesame seeds piled
the same way they fell last time you shook it.

You on a subway platform:
Red lipstick, bleached white shirt,
and gelled-back, brown nazi-do.
But it's not you.

On a gray tar road, a white line—that's you—between arriving and
      departing.

A woman who reminds me of you flirts.
When she says my name it spills into one of the moats dug in me by
      your voice.
How am I doing? Volcanic feathers flickering in and out of sleep.

10:01

The clock at my bedside would clack too loudly for you, so I'd move and cover it, make like it wasn't there.

Tonight my head brittle as a leaf, weak as a child leaving the bubby.

•

My body followed my parents. Bubby, pigeon-toed, came after us with a helium grin.

On the outside corner of her eyes islands of raised skin pink as a jammed thumb, flaps on a rooster's head.

•

Funnels of gray swoop me inside.

Fear my future is the dankness that clings to Bubby like her dress;
fear the funnel's vortex is wind pinned into everyone's pocket, let
loose when we grow up.

•

Is Bubby dying, now? She sits every day in one of those chiclet-
colored chairs surrounding the nurses' station, where they serve pills
in Italian ice cups. Sticks to her rule never to talk to old people and
goyim. Her eyes, red-rimmed, drainy as raw egg white.

At home, she'd sit on a bench in front of her building all day, always
alive and dying.

•

Close my eyes,
graze your hip.
Sinuous.

Inches from you
fingers extend
smooth, into

a field

Stub of a melted candle,
I don't burn tonight
as I think of you knit to another.

•

Bob of a field mouse, Bubby's stretched black pumps, a bulging
tire, my clock.

I'm wearing my pajamas with the solar system on them.

12:43. Fear I'm of a species that opens over and over, withering
before it blossoms

ex-utero

my body   a sunray   diagonal   on a stone sundial
carved in/on ground
found myself   in some aztec(?) courtyard   when i awake
my bed   the sundial   my body   a sun ray

what time is it?   in/on the
circle of getting over   past her
somewhere   in the middle

ahead etchless stone
when shadow marks
end

          *

when I think of her
I see the curve of a melon.
flesh tipped forward,
the seeds stripped out,
hung together with goo.

and a braid, blonde:
a *havdallah* candle,
the twist of dusk, sun
going, a landscape
blackening

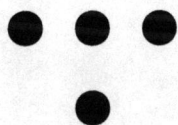

The Moon Is an Antiseptic in Your Religion.

When I open black clear down to its neck,
              and glide it onto a hanger,   it falls

in the shape of a swan.

Autobiography

I was afraid my life would be like visiting my grandparents
when I was little: green carpet, big ugly sofas, and no one
having anything to say; my grandfather seeming not to
be thinking; no one wanting to talk to anyone,
just no one having anything to say. Sitting there
like mummies, out of duty, no other reason.
I sit and look straight at the hollowness: a bullseye.

I want to say my life has
been a pipecleaner, beautifully twisted,
in tandem with others like it.

Or, not beautiful, a known-by-name shape;
nothing to do but let the form of things take over.

Like the signature of a bald tree stump

. . . about impressions,
how they're shed, picked over;
notations for

what's strange.

Next thing I knew you were sealed in a Ziploc bag
            for good.
Your argument about solipsism, like coke,
being *the only real thing*,
faded.

We're no more responsible for our dreams
than a pond is for its reflections.

. . . white text sinks into water
.sduolc eht htiw derhs I

Desire like the wind out back that rustles the leaves.
I'd rather play with a ghost than all alone.

Up the Wazoo River

I think I know the precise extent of my desires, i.e.: half a banana,
    please.
This makes me not even want the damn banana.

The big deal thing was finding I had moved while eating, I wanted
    the whole banana.
Like the buildings in midtown, blinding in their fixity until I spot
    shadows snaking across them.

       Suppose glass crush envelope sees all the way back
       while cherries back the door in antelope fur
       dark green slide
       Hemlines scatter towards ants
       Lean apples spar across planks.

Tootsie, it'll cost you $. Have I made myself clear?
Cold voice shaking dewdrops. Take it east of the stringbean.
Static ahem ahem Amen.

Gesture

A compelling need to turn someone's deficiencies into musical notes/
The needle is the haystack.

I watched you repose like the majestic heron:
As if we, together, made a marshland.

You have a squeaky voice; aether.
Overall, there is a lightness to

You, a quiver in the wind,

That's why you twitch often
When out at sea, intimate sea,

You transpose into a sail—

It's the fastest way to move into distance.

U

Reaching into the bottle's mouth; gullet.

Very tiny bottle.

Like a vault,

like a pleased mouth.

Upside-down breast.

The thing I would hold in my hand.

Its neck, Modigliani. A stick slanted in its gullet.

Smooth glass.

A reflection like a window. Tiny.

The glass bottle from an upside-down breast to a house.

The upsidedown breast turns into a suction cup.

Used to attach things to a window: memorabilia,

or something stained-glass, perhaps.

Incense not the right perfume now, the smell coasts with associations.
    Want to sleep. When someone

talks, want to strangle them. Am a sucker for tenderness, delicacy.

Ovule

A sunflower seed
hulled,
a tear

pinioned between two fingers;

the shade of barked tree,
bone.

·

You have a tip like the citron
pointed during *Succoth* to the four directions:
two poles, sunrise, and sunset.

A tip like a nipple, bird beak, tooth,
but I know it's your navel,

and where an umbilical root might have rested
along the center of your underbelly

is now a crook;

if you were a boat,
passengers would sit in this scar.

Patriarch Sky

Just for the hell of it,
you took out scissors
and cut up the sky.
Mostly clipped shapes
of the svelte female hip,
water jugs,
Cheshire leers,
grinning way the blades opened
and closed.

Loose raiments curled, torn, wrung,
flying
limp as old bed linen kids jump on,
ripping when the wind blows.

This is what's left of my
ceiling,
helter-skelter
puzzle,
mansion of the mind.

slip

She thought they were accidents. The red peel next to the green avocado looked promising. The house, though, was in bad shape. Very dilapidated. "Stand at the window!" he called to her. "Oh, dear," she sighed, "my persimmon is overripe." On the verge of something, she thought. But what?, she asked. It kept going up and down. As long as the children were okay, so were the parents. They never wanted it to be this way. Who would have? The green in the salad was invisible. The red, however, stood out. More and more, she wanted to see. How things turned out the way they did. Her throat itched. She was cracking off the top of some celery. Without passion she loved. The red pepper in the bowl caught her attention. "Oh, why me," she sighed. The sweater at her wrist looked like leg warmers on an ankle. She heard a sound, like tin hitting porcelain. The new soap dish falling off the side of the tub again, she imagined. She made herself a note to buy beets.

Poem for my mother who wishes she were a lilypad
in a Monet painting

We're in a gray tree (you and I).
Lunging into an orange—not eating it.

I'd like nothing better than to come to another kind of arrangement;
mostly, though, we just don't come apart.

,

Behold
a single contractual mark
to possess and to withhold (contractions),
and the dialogue within the dialogue that began before it.

Black seeds on a white dish
.... (pores)

The sound of your voice has always been a fragment

                organized as a flower,
        a tin can clingclanging upstream,

the spaces between my heartbeats
        lengthening (like shadows);

You a part of the tough rubbery vine that expands on the skin of the
        pond.

Celerity

After a pot of smoked tea I drink trees. Green there
orange here yellow. Leaves now triangles then
grapes; round, fleshy pulses of color. Through
butternut leaves (feet playing crackles like fingers
on a flute), themselves moonlike, that bed on a
lake's rim. Lakewater a newly-minted penny.
Pumpkin-gold across everything. In a short time it's
bottom-naked in a glass. 6PM. Thick light sucked
up quickly, as if through a straw.

up quickly, as if through a straw.
bottom-naked in a glass. 6PM. Thick light sucked
Pumpkin-gold across everything. In a short time it's
lake's rim. Lakewater a newly-minted penny.
on a flute), themselves moonlike, that bed on a
butternut leaves (feet playing crackles like fingers
grapes; round, fleshy pulses of color. Through
orange here yellow. Leaves now triangles then
After a pot of smoked tea I drink trees. Green there

Babble

Suddenly I'm let out.

Something

first: images

rinse me in their saliva

the way a cat licks itself clean,

section by section.

It's a matter of hygiene to know who you are.

Did you notice someone plucking

a few air-dried things

off the clothesline for you, out back?

A barely noticeable line flickers past.

Morning sprouts heads and tails

like cut earthworms.

Loss

Crisscrossing flesh voice
I am guilty—I am guilty—I am

Bird-pecked overripe berries
Lie scattered on the ground. Falling
Parenthesis,
Little arcs,
Inflamed & stoplight

Saying something
Makes a curve (skirt)
In the line of.

Again a voice draws overhead.
             Sorry & sour
             The miscellaneous chunks of;

lasso.

Cornucopia

A harvest of gourds
piles up around my collar,
tumbling from my head
as if it's a basket.

Their demented shapes,
green with splats of sun,
sprout
as I exit the elevator.

This morning on the subway
I was trying to twist my life
to fit me, a delicate activity.
I saw the Tree

in the Garden of Chaos.
Then, my small brother's old ghost and I,
swinging high in its branches, the sky a book,
and my feet turning its pages to the blanks after the end.

Still Life of a Woman

Helen Keller used scent like a yarn to measure distance.
When I smoke cigarettes, space elongates.
I live within mesh.
A cat squawks.

At eight, loneliness is a Western: horses stampeding across the Old
      Frontier,
kicking up a lot of dust.
The family is wandering:
Father busying himself with the mechanics of the wagon,
Mother,

theme song: "Girls Just Want to Have Fun"(only it's 1966).
No; Mother is both the tinkling of a chandelier and the light refracting.

For someone who has lived mostly celibate,
there is music—tones like pressure on almost-ice water
packaged in see-through plastic—
ripples like sunlight and shadows of branches and leaves.
For someone who has lived mostly celibate,
there is music—
Is sex a sense?
If so, do the other senses get keener to compensate? One could say
      they dull.
. . . But if one is always wanting?

My bark turns gray.
August, the harvest moon sags.
This the only August I will be forty.

There is no child.
A part of me is dying, I would like to say.

A Thin Green Line

The classic scientific approach: develop new representations that enable you to see a clear picture . . .

The night hikes me up on its shoulders.
Want to bear back, far inward,
not like a plant.   clover   cactus   gas   glass   sage   sea foam
stem   little men   snowpeas
grasshopper   ever
verdureverdureverdureverdureverdureverdureverdureverdure (proceed)
tea   agree   algae   envy   ivy
    army   aloe   avocado
Dino   pistachio   Osiris   mucus   cumin   cucumber
caterpillar   lilypad   pine   thyme   vine
      lime   slime
unseasoned   inside of a kiwi/
               a pond
jade   slate   fennel   vernal   fertile   beryl   bile
crocodile   kelly   Comet   Kermit   corporate
parrot   scarab   bulb
shrubs or trees (depending on your height)
Knight   hepatitis   highway exits
watercress   skin stain after wearing some metal-backed jewelry
the ray   Beret   Bay   -brier common in Europe   thumb
      Mountains
mint   viridis   lettuce   turtle   astroturf
    "Tropicana"
public mailboxes that are private
root   Kool   toothpaste   Old High German gruoni
Gumbie   Old Saxon groni   garden hose   groen (700)
olive oil
    chlorophyll
LaCrosse   X-mas   Venus   sprouts   -house   -est   -backs

card   chalkboard   park bench
-wich   -ish   -er   ore   raw   originally zro
(*walk*)   watermelon rind   Modern German grün
unlit tv screen   (1150) Old English grene   penicillium
naive   vein   chives
unlucky to Scots   pot   traffic control box   American Express   moss

to increase in size by assimilation of material into living organism or
          by accretion
                    of material in a   nonbiological process   (as
                         crystallization)
                                   to assume some relation through, or as if
                                   through

          Old Frisian gréne
grape leaves   pumpkin seeds   "1-Hour Parking"   garbage bags for
          recycling
Tonka trucks   imperial color of the Aztecs
7-up   seaweed   sunglasses   subway line   bice
the numbers branded into an arm
to pass into a condition
Hibernia
in its present form since the 15th Century   secondary
in jail lingo, target for death   wheatgrass
hydrous arsenite of copper   emerald   blind to red and
fluorescent silk from a silkworm engineered in 1999 by inserting a
          jellyfish gene that produces a fluorescent protein

viridity

smell   freshly tilled earth   viscous   punctured
I divide in its wound   grow into   become

                    *

A green thought in a green shade

Pitch the shadow as if it were a tent,
Prop open.

Turn back a cloud,
Fold some water.

On the horizon hang
Birds who neigh.

Blisters of yellow and blue, then
Daffodils smothering the ink.

Start over.

Pitch the shadow against a wall.
Red showers like lice.

Pitch the shadow to its voice.
Pitch the shadow

        *

Four days before the equinox—
St. Patrick's day, my father's birthday;

Flash, and so forth
Through the throng
On their way home
After the parade.
Fermented father   Patri   a combining form borrowed from
Latin patri- from pater   Green
fathers

Thus began my exploration of green.

*Ambiguous Loss   when the lost person is still physically present but
emotionally absent often helped just by knowing there is a name for the
problem*

And what about ire?

Flight

Different points of view
scattered all over the globe
are called to a meeting. Like distant relatives
who haven't seen each other in ages, some now have families
of their own. They arrive mid-sentence,
wearing various outfits depending on whether they had been playing
tennis, etc.

I herd them around a circle,
talk with purpose like a scout leader to cubs.
There's been a major change
in outlook. What was private, secret, and silent.
A red ink drawing of a horse pulls a chariot uphill.

     The product is the pulley.

Only in the virginal sky between the lattice of lines
does one not get tramelled.
How to turn one's self harmless.

Poem

I touched where I thought the piano started and either it was a white glove or a curtain blowing, but this shine of light in the shape of an object landed across the keys I was playing, and then I went blind. It was a dark room to begin with—plush red carpet, black piano, and I had dark hair. I felt for the bench I was sitting on

Blue Skies

It's a new sky today. I want to use this blue to make.
New, as we call the moon when it isn't visible,
but here, black smoke instead of the moon.

I want to take the blue like it's something.
Today the most beautiful blue ever.
The fullest range of shades I want to list them.
Blue alone a rainbow.

On the third day, gone the smoke to breathe from,
gone the black funnel to a hovering
like a swarm;
a net, perhaps, of a yellowing black that makes me think of
someone dead, so, perhaps, the flag of corpse.

Today no interference.
You can keep looking up the blue.

Only across town the still-fresh smell,
guttural blue.

A Ritual

1.

Today was going to email: *amethyst, jade, ivory,*
but why seduce with pictures when sex is out of the question.

A diet of e's: I'd e you an image first thing in the morning.
Eventually you'd pick out feelings with a toothpick, leaving a rind.
I learned to send scintillating rinds.

What a life: 10 a.m. at my computer station, click *on*, abuzz
for the chime and blinking white apple, your
name, and an image-package to unwrap.
Packages several times a day,
interrupting our jobs in screenlight
 the taste of aspirin dissolving, light-powder
accreting quickly into a chalky cast
coating our bodies, white flesh instead of sound.

2.

All day sky turns shades of soil.
After work, home and wait for rain.
Turn up Bach crescendo, clear the windows
to watch the nerve expose;
it's summer, and everyone expects a maniacal storm
after air so thick it's presence.

Lunchtime, the presence felt like a lover relieving your absence

I leave a bone unturned,

wait for rain:

thunder, small vessels breaking.
slow storm, drizzle.

No rain in Brooklyn that night, but in Millerton, New York,
electricity gets knocked out.

3.

Weekend morning, a Bonnard-shimmer through the window,
        shavings from all our descriptions;
letters are colors, temperature, smell

                *

An end happens *right now,* but the event is a distant point like
starlight, taking a certain
        equation of time to travel before reaching

                *

You're hidden like Jonah: open my mouth, eject you whole.

                *

I leave bouquets out in the sun,
incantations to return you to the unknown.
But first I roam—*where, where*—*on this grass, that patch?*

                *

One on either end,
two sparrows hold a robe in their beaks.

This is the robe of loss,
the wind creates a gully in the fabric.

acknowledgements

thank you to the editors of the following journals in which some of these poems first appeared, sometimes in slightly different forms:

Afterthoughts: 'Getting Closer to the Big Bang'
American Letters & Commentary: 'Celerity'
Aufgabe: 'A Thin Green Line'
Barrow Street: 'Numbness and shade'
Black Zinnias: 'Poem'
Can We Have Our Ball Back?: 'Ovule,' 'Babble'
Chelsea: 'Poem for my mother who wishes she were a lilypad,'
      'To the New Lover'
The Evergreen Chronicles: 'A Series of Seven,' 'Birdsong'
Field: 'spoke'
Greatcoat: 'Loss,' 'Cornucopia,' 'The Moon Is an Antiseptic in your Religion.'
Illuminations: 'Still Life of a Woman'
The Journal: 'Limn'
La Fovea: 'Up the Wazoo River'
Luna°: '-TUDE'
Modern Words: 'ex-utero'
No Exit: 'Rorschach'
Painted Bride Quarterly: 'The Grasses Unload their Grief'
Paragraph: 'slip'
Phoebe: 'The Importance of Being Earnest'
Salamander: 'Here'
Salt Hill Journal: 'Gesture'
6ix: 'The Night Is My Purse/and Here's What I Empty Out:,'
Seneca Review: 'Flight'
Storyscape: 'Photographs'
13th Moon: 'The Wind of Madness Has Broken a Skin'
Web del Sol: 'The Existing Lover in Everyday Life,' 'Waving,' 'Origami'
Western Humanities Review: 'Chantilly Lace'

'Blue Skies' received The Poetry Society of America's Lyric Poem Award, and aired on National Public Radio.

'A Thin Green Line' was finalist for The Poetry Society of America's Cecil Hemley Memorial Award.

'The Grasses Unload Their Grief' received *Painted Bride Quarterly*'s Poetry Prize.

'Celerity' was featured on *Poetry Daily*'s website.

'Chantilly Lace' was the runner-up for *Western Humanities Review*'s Utah Writers' Award.

'Poem for my mother who wishes she were a lilypad in a Monet painting' also appears in *Letters to the World: Poems from the WOM-PO Listserv* (Red Hen Press, 2008).

the author would like to express gratitude to the Ragdale Foundation, the Vermont Studio Center, and the MacDowell Arts Colony for providing the time and space to write and revise some of these poems.

•

thank you to the numerous friends, fellow writers, and teachers over the years for their insightful reading and/or encouragement, humor, and support during this book's many phases and faces in its colorful odyssey to find a home: Rebecca Acker, L.S. Asekoff, Geoffrey Babbitt, Arthur Berger, Donna Cartelli, Jill Dawsey, Danielle Deulen, Craig Dworkin, Cornelius Eady, Elaine Equi, Helen Ruth Freeman, Barbara Guest, Lauren Huber, Maureen Kennedy, Stacy Kidd, Matthew Kirkpatrick, Kirsten Jorgensen, Kristin Hatch, Lois Hirshkowitz, Kimberly Lojeck, Pepper Luboff, Hermine Meinhard, Katrinka Moore, Bonnie Oglensky, Cami Nelson, Molly Peacock, Robert Pinsky, Joan Lauri Poole, D.A. Powell, Liz Poreba, Donna Ratajczak, Nicole Sheets, Brenda Sieczkowski, Sarah Stern, Stephanie Strickland, Isaac Sullivan, Cole Swensen, Jackie Tierney, Jean Valentine, G.C. Waldrep, Elisabeth Whitehead, Holly Welker, and Dean Young—— & to my friends and fellow writers for their keen feedback and encouragement while these poems were being written: Julie Carr, Guillermo Filice Castro, Val Clark, Ron Drummond, Katie Johntz, Sharon Krauss, Amy Lemmon, Martie McCleery Palar, Evelyn Reilly, and Yerra Sugarman. a shout-out to Irene Schaller for printing countless manuscript submissions when I didn't have access to a sturdy-enough printer!

profound appreciation to Marjorie Welish for choosing 'A Thin Green Line' for PSA's Cecil Hemley Memorial Award, as well as to Mark Levine for choosing 'Blue Skies' for PSA's Lyric Poem Award, and to Carole Oles for choosing 'The Grasses Unload Their Grief' for *Painted Bride Quarterly*'s Poetry Prize.

thanks to the writing community at the University of Utah for their good spirit and encouragement, and special thanks to Ely Shipley, Christine Marshall, and Nathan Hauke for their sensitive re-re-reading and cheer when these poems were already grown. thanks most especially to Phillis Levin for her critical guidance, inspiration, and appreciation when many of these poems first germinated; to Jacqueline Osherow, Karen Brennan, and Donald Revell for reinspiration. muchas gracias to Jessica Treat for her friendship, imagination, and belief throughout.

enormous thanks to my editor, Tony Frazer, for my first book, and for making it possible for me to finally give my thanks to all these people.

Shira Dentz is the author of a forthcoming book of poetry, *door of thin skins* (CavanKerry Press), and a chapbook, *Leaf Weather* (Tilt Press). Her poems and stories have appeared in many journals including *The American Poetry Review, The Iowa Review, Western Humanities Review, jubilat, Brooklyn Rail, The Black Warrior Review,* and *Bombay Gin,* and have been featured on *Poetry Daily* and National Public Radio. She is the recipient of an Academy of American Poets' Prize, The Poetry Society of America's Lyric Poem Award and Cecil Hemely Memorial Award, *Painted Bride Quarterly*'s Poetry Prize, and *Electronic Poetry Review*'s Discovery Award. She is a graduate of the Iowa Writers' Workshop, and currently is Poetry Co-editor of *Quarterly West,* a Fellow at the Tanner Center for the Humanities in Salt Lake City, and is finishing a Ph.D. in literature and creative writing at the University of Utah. Before leaving for Iowa City and Salt Lake City, she worked for many years as a graphic artist designing music ads in New York City, and taught English in an inner city public high school. This is her first book.

www.ingramcontent.com/pod-product-compliance
Lightning Source LLC
Chambersburg PA
CBHW022201080426
42734CB00006B/534